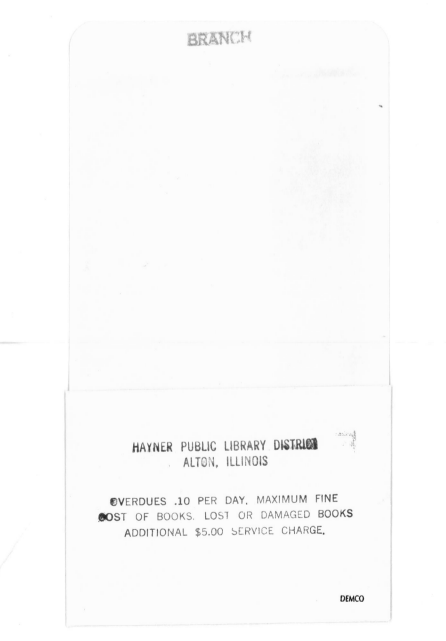

20th Century Inventions
ROCKETS AND SPACECRAFT

Robert Snedden

RSVP
RAINTREE
STECK-VAUGHN
PUBLISHERS
The Steck-Vaughn Company

Austin, Texas

20th Century Inventions

AIRCRAFT

CARS

COMPUTERS

THE DIGITAL REVOLUTION

THE INTERNET

LASERS

MEDICAL ADVANCES

NUCLEAR POWER

ROCKETS AND SPACECRAFT

SATELLITES

TELECOMMUNICATIONS

Front cover and title page: The space shuttle lifts off on another mission into space.

Published by Raintree Steck-Vaughn Publishers, an imprint of Steck-Vaughn Company

Library of Congress Cataloging-in-Publication Data
Snedden, Robert.
Rockets and spacecraft / Robert Snedden.
    p.   cm.—(20th century inventions)
    Includes bibliographical references and index.
    Summary: Surveys the technological changes that have taken place during our exploration of space, discussing missiles, space stations, the space shuttle, and other developments.
    ISBN 0-8172-4817-X
    1. Astronautics—Juvenile literature.
    2. Rockets (Aeronautics)—Juvenile literature.
    3. Space vehicles—Juvenile literature.
    [1. Space vehicles. 2. Astronautics. 3. Outer space—Exploration]
    I. Title. II. Series.
    TL793.S62   1998
    629.4—dc21   97-28059

Printed in Italy. Bound in the United States.
1 2 3 4 5 6 7 8 9 0 01 00 99 98 97

Picture acknowledgments
Mary Evans Picture Library 4, 6 (both). Genesis Space Photo Library front cover and title page/NASA, 17 (bottom), 19 (top), 25, 26 (left), 27 (both)/NASA, 35/NASA, 39, 40, 43. The Image Bank 28. Science Photo Library back cover and 3/David A. Hardy, 5/David Ducros for ESA, 10/David A. Hardy, 11/NASA, 23/Erik Viktor, 24 (both)/Novosti, 29/NASA, 38/Don Davis, NASA, 41/Jinsei Chyo/NASDA, 42/Space Telescope Science Institute/NASA. TRH Pictures 8 (right), 15/CASA, 18, 19 (bottom)/USAF, 20/USAF, 21/DOD, 30/MatraBAe Dynamics, 32, 33 (top)/Euromissile, 33 (bottom)/MDC, 34/NASA. Artwork on pages 13, 14, 17, 36–37 by Tim Benké, Top Draw (Tableaux). All other pictures Wayland Picture Library.

CONTENTS

INTRODUCTION

Around the middle of the twelfth century, someone in China had an idea that would one day change the world and the way we see it. He took a firework and tied it to an arrow. When he lit the firework, the arrow shot into the air. The rocket had been born.

Today, 800 years later, rockets have taken us farther and faster than those people could ever have imagined. Rockets have allowed people to walk on the moon and sent probes to the outer reaches of the solar system. But they are also among the most powerful of the weapons available to the world's armed forces. Aircraft, ground troops, and ships are all equipped with rockets and, despite the end of the Cold War, there are still hundreds of nuclear-tipped intercontinental ballistic missiles (ICBMs) in submarines and underground missile sites.

The Chinese were the first to discover the explosive nature of gunpowder. They also had the inspired idea of using it to propel missiles through the air.

The European Space Agency (ESA) *Ariane 5* rocket is used to place satellites in earth orbit. Today, rocket launches are so common that they scarcely get mentioned on television news programs.

It was the search for military supremacy that spurred on rocket development. In World War II (1939–1945), the Germans developed their rocket program as a means of attacking targets their aircraft could no longer reach. *Sputnik 1*, the first satellite, was launched by the Soviet Union using a modified ICBM, as were the first United States astronauts. Even the space shuttle, although not strictly a military vehicle, has flown entirely military missions, putting spy satellites into orbit.

While there will always be those who see the rocket as a weapon of destruction, there are many others who see it as a way of opening up the "final frontier" beyond the earth, expanding our horizons out into the universe.

FIRE IN THE SKY

We do not know who the first rocketeer was, but in 1232, the Chinese fought off a Mongol attack at the town of Kai-fung-fu by showering them with "arrows of flaming fire." The propellant, or fuel, for these early rockets was a form of gunpowder, which produced a fiery exhaust and "a noise like thunder." By the beginning of the fifteenth century, the Chinese had multiple rocket launchers mounted on wheelbarrows and two-stage rockets that could release a swarm of rocket arrows at a target more than a mile (1.6 km) away.

The Arabs, who had trading links with the Chinese, are thought to have introduced the rocket to Europe in the thirteenth century. By the sixteenth century, every European army had its rocket corps, since rockets had longer ranges than the firearms of the time. As firearms improved, rockets were less widely used, although they did not disappear from the battlefield entirely.

Science-fiction rockets

In 1865, Jules Verne produced his famous novel, *From the Earth to the Moon*. In it, he described using a giant cannon to shoot people to the moon from Florida. Coincidentally, Verne's lunar travelers took off from a spot not too far from Cape Canaveral, where the United States' Apollo missions to the moon would later be launched. A few years later, Edward Everett Hale published a story that described a habitable earth satellite. Imaginations were being fired by the possibilities that rockets offered.

Jules Verne (1828–1905) was one of the fathers of the science fiction novel. His intrepid explorers (left) take a stroll on the moon, seemingly unconcerned by the lack of air to breathe.

The rockets' red glare

In the eighteenth century, the British in India saw what rockets could do when they were attacked and defeated several times by the rocket corps of the Indian rulers Hyder Ali and his son, Tippu Sultan. On one occasion, flights of 2,000 rockets were volleyed at the British.

The British themselves had some success in improving the range and accuracy of rockets. William Congreve produced a faster-burning powder and made improvements to their design and manufacture. His rockets were just over 3 feet (1m) in length with 15-foot (4.5-m) balancing sticks—like giant fireworks rockets. They had a range of almost 2 miles (3km). They were first used in battle in 1806, in an attack on Napoleon's fleet.

Rockets were also fired against United States troops in an attack on Fort McHenry at Baltimore in 1814. The reference to "the rockets' red glare" in the national anthem, "The Star-Spangled Banner," is a description of the bombardment.

By 1844, William Hale, another Englishman, had invented rockets that spun as they flew, like rifle bullets. They were made to spin by deflecting the exhaust through nozzles drilled in the rocket's baseplate. This gave them greater stability and meant they no longer needed the unwieldy balancing sticks.

Firing rockets, an idea the British learned in India, was a technique used against Napoleon's forces at the Battle of Waterloo in 1815.

FROM IMAGINATION TO REALITY

Robert Goddard (second from the left) was one of the pioneers of modern rocketry. The picture below shows the successful launch of one his many rocket designs.

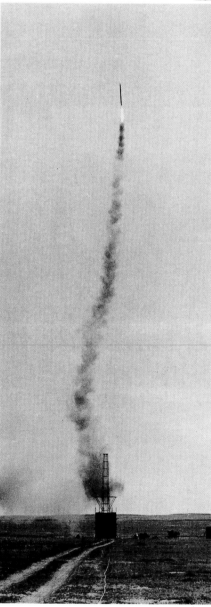

Three men were largely responsible for the birth of the modern rocket: the Russian Konstantin E. Tsiolkovsky (1857–1935), the Transylvanian-German Hermann Oberth (1894–1989), and the American Robert H. Goddard (1882–1945). Working independently, they developed the fundamental principles of rocket action and how it might be used to escape the earth's gravity for flight in space.

Tsiolkovsky, a Russian schoolteacher, produced papers in 1903 describing how rockets could be used for space exploration and how spinning space-habitats with artificial gravity could be made.

In 1919, Robert Goddard published a booklet called *A Method of Reaching Extreme Altitude,* which explored the possibility of using rocket-powered vehicles to send scientific instruments into the stratosphere. He even considered that a very large rocket might be able to put scientific instruments on the surface of the moon. Goddard was ridiculed for suggesting such a "fantastic" thing.

In March 1926, Goddard flew the world's first liquid-propellant rocket on the Ward Farm near Auburn in Massachusetts. Local fire marshals were alarmed by his activities and banned any further rocket experiments. He moved to Roswell in New Mexico, where he developed the first gyro-controlled rocket-guidance system. Goddard took out over 200 patents on rockets and space-flight devices.

German rocketeers

In Germany, Hermann Oberth published *The Rocket Into Interplanetary Space* in 1923. His work inspired a group of budding rocketeers who, in 1932, went to work for the German army at Kummersdorf near Berlin. The German army had been banned from having long-range artillery after World War I (1914–1918) and was interested in the possibilities of having rockets as replacements.

In 1937, the group, led by Werner von Braun, set up a research center at Peenemünde. Here, von Braun and his team perfected a series of liquid-propellant rocket vehicles. Eventually, they built the famous V-2, the world's first long-range ballistic missile. It was used with devastating effect in the closing stages of World War II.

At the end of the war, the Peenemünde research center was captured by the Soviet forces, along with many of the German rocket engineers. Von Braun and his development team surrendered to the U.S. army and he was brought to the United States in 1946. He played a crucial role in the development of the U.S. space program.

Werner von Braun (pointing), one of the masterminds of the Apollo moon program, was also responsible for the V2 rockets that brought terror to Great Britain at the end of World War II (above).

A ROCKET EXPLOSION

Sputnik 1, the first artificial satellite to orbit the earth. It carried no scientific instruments, just a simple radio transmitter that allowed scientists to track its orbit. The name means "fellow traveler" in Russian.

The rocket research and development that had begun during World War II continued after the war. In the second half of the 1950s, the USSR and the United States succeeded in using German equipment and skill to develop the ICBM. The liquid-propellant rocket motors developed for the ICBMs were powerful enough to open up the possibility of space flight.

The Space Age began in 1957, when the USSR launched *Sputnik I*. From then on, the technology of rocket engines developed rapidly. Small liquid-fuel thrusters that could reliably be fired, shut down, and fired again as required were produced, allowing a spacecraft to be maneuvered accurately in flight.

At the other end of the scale was the mighty F–1 engine, developed as part of the Apollo moon landings program. Five of these engines, each one large enough for a person to walk around in, were used to provide the thrust needed to lift the giant Saturn V rocket into space. Each F–1 developed over 1,500,000 pounds (680,000 kg) of thrust.

Breakthroughs were also made in the construction of fuel tanks that could hold liquid oxygen and hydrogen, which have to be kept at very low temperatures. Protective materials for heat shields were also developed.

At the same time, research continued into the more economical solid-fuel rocket engines. Solid fuel had some advantages over liquid fuel. It was particularly useful for short-range battlefield rockets and in anti-missile systems, since they could be made ready to fire in a shorter time.

The powerful Saturn V rocket that propelled the Apollo missions to the moon.

Spectacular successes

Within twenty years of the launch of *Sputnik 1*, rockets had led to spectacular successes in space exploration. Fleets of satellites traveled in orbit, mapping the earth's surface, sending communications from continent to continent, observing the rest of the universe, and spying on the people below. Probes flew to almost every other planet in the solar system and even landed on some of them. Most spectacularly of all, twelve men walked on the moon.

The biggest drawback of a rocket such as the Saturn V is its cost and wastefulness. It can only be fired once and is then discarded. Today, the search is for efficiency. Small, easy-to-maintain rockets that can be refueled and relaunched are needed. With private companies and individuals competing to be the first to send someone into space cheaply, a new age of space travel for all may be about to begin.

FOR EVERY ACTION . . .

Newton's Third Law of Motion

The great scientist Sir Isaac Newton (1642–1727) set out the basic laws of motion. His third law explains the working principle behind the rocket. It says:

For every action, there is an equal and opposite reaction.

In other words, if you push against something, it pushes you back. If you try pushing hard against a wall, you move back. That is because the wall is much more massive than you are. If you push something small, like a plate, there is still a force pushing back at you, but it is so small you scarcely notice. It does not take much effort to push your plate away after a meal.

How does a rocket actually work? Although it can be very powerful, a rocket is actually one of the simplest of all engines. Unlike an aircraft or car engine, a rocket carries its own "air" in the form of an oxidizer. This is a chemical that supplies oxygen. Without oxygen, combustion cannot take place. The oxidizer, together with the fuel, are the propellants (see page 16). The fuel and oxidizer are burned together in a combustion chamber and this produces hot gases that reach a temperature of around 5,000° F (2,800° C).

Sir Isaac Newton was one of the world's greatest thinkers.

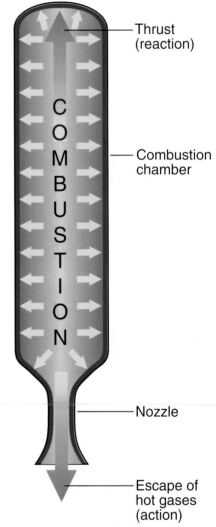

Thrust (reaction)

Combustion chamber

COMBUSTION

Nozzle

Escape of hot gases (action)

In the combustion chamber, hot gases are produced by burning fuel. The gases are allowed to escape through a nozzle that points in the opposite direction from the one in which the rocket travels. The thrust produced by the combustion of the fuel propels the rocket forward.

The molecules that make up the gases have a lot of energy. Inside the combustion chamber they push in all directions against the walls. If the chamber were sealed and strong enough to contain the gases, all these forces would be balanced and the rocket would not move. However, in the rocket engine, the gases are allowed to escape at high speed through a nozzle. This causes an imbalance in the forces inside the chamber. The pressure exerted on the rocket in the forward direction is now much greater than the pressure exerted in the backward direction. The result is that the rocket shoots forward.

The rocket is obeying Newton's third law of motion. The escaping exhaust gases are the action, and the forward pressure, or thrust, is the reaction. The same principle applies to other types of rockets, such as electric and nuclear rockets that expel charged particles or even beams of light. All are able to operate both within the earth's atmosphere and in the near-vacuum of space. A rocket can work anywhere. In fact, it works best in a vacuum because there are no air molecules to get in the way of the escaping gases.

PROPELLANTS

The test firing of a space shuttle solid-fuel booster. The booster is designed to be recovered and reused after each shuttle launch.

Solid propellants

Fireworks, the very first rockets, used a solid propellant in the form of gunpowder. Solid-fuel rockets are the easiest to make and are by far the simplest in construction. In a solid-propellant rocket engine, the combustion chamber and the propellant storage tank are combined in one unit. The propellants are in solid form, usually already mixed together, and they are placed right in the combustion chamber itself. There is no need for a mechanism to inject the propellants continuously into a combustion chamber from storage tanks, as there is with a liquid-fuel rocket (see page 16). The solid propellant is simply ignited and burns until it is used up.

A solid propellant burns only on its surface, and so the shape of the propellant can be designed to set the rate at which the fuel is consumed. This allows the thrust of the rocket to be determined in advance. Solid-fuel rocket engines can be designed to give continuous steady thrust, a steadily increasing thrust, or a steadily decreasing thrust, according to the way the fuel is burned.

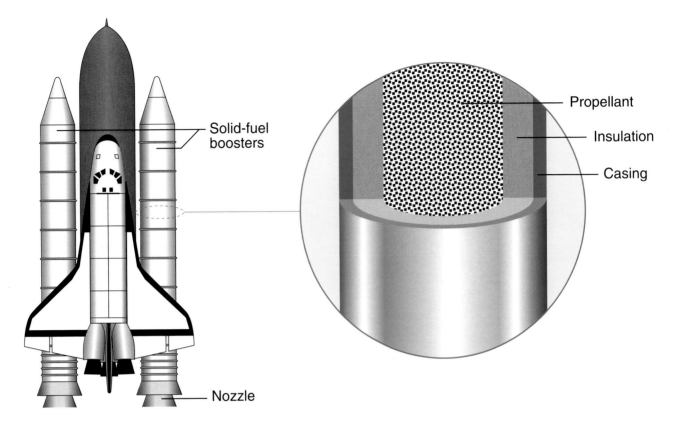

Solid-fuel boosters

Propellant

Insulation

Casing

Nozzle

There are several combinations of chemicals that are suitable for use as solid propellants. The two main types of solid propellant, double-base propellants and composite propellants, were first developed fifty years ago and are still widely used. Double-base propellants consist chiefly of a blend of nitrocellulose and nitroglycerine with small quantities of other materials to control the burning rate. They are ignited by a blast from a small chemical igniter. However, they can become less reliable with age, so artillery rockets made with these propellants can be stored for only a limited time. Composite propellants are mixtures of an oxidizer, usually a chemical such as ammonium chlorate, set within a solid hydrocarbon fuel.

Although they do not provide as much energy as a similar weight of a good liquid propellant, solid propellants have the advantages of fast ignition and being easier to store in the rocket. Their manufacture can, however, be a costly and hazardous process. The space shuttle boosters are a good example of modern solid-fuel rockets—they use the chemical aluminum perchlorate as the oxidizer and powdered aluminum as the fuel.

The space shuttle launcher combines both solid- and liquid-fuel engines. The solid-fuel boosters provide the additional power needed to propel the shuttle through the dense lower layers of the earth's atmosphere.

LIQUID PROPELLANTS

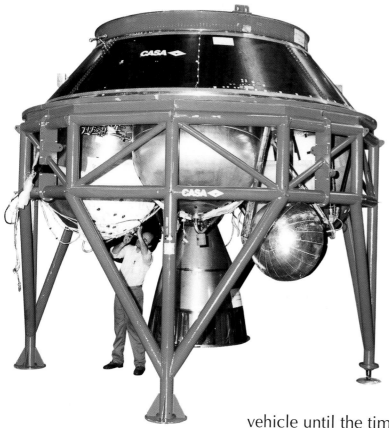

Part of the liquid-fueled upper-stage assembly of an *Ariane 5* rocket.

Most rockets use liquid propellants, since these can provide more energy and therefore more thrust than solid propellants. They also have the advantage that the thrust can be controlled by adjusting the amount of propellant sent into the combustion chamber. Liquid-fuel rockets can be divided into two types. Bipropellant rockets carry the fuel and the oxidizer in separate tanks and bring them together in the combustion chamber. Monopropellant rockets are fueled by a single liquid that is both an oxidizer and a fuel.

Large fuel tanks are needed to store the liquid propellants within the rocket vehicle until the time comes to introduce them into the combustion chamber of the rocket engine. Once combustion has started, pressure builds up inside the chamber and the propellants will no longer flow into it. This means that there has to be some way of forcing the propellants into the combustion chamber against the pressure resulting from the combustion process. The simpler of the two methods used to deal with this problem involves using a gas, such as helium, to force the propellants out of the tanks and into the combustion chamber.

In the second method, pumps are used to draw the propellants from the tanks and force them into the combustion chamber. These pumps are usually driven by a turbine powered by a small device called a gas generator. The propellants are driven into the combustion chamber through an injector. The injector is perforated with hundreds of tiny holes, like a large shower head. It breaks up the propellants into a fine spray, ensuring a good mix and complete combustion.

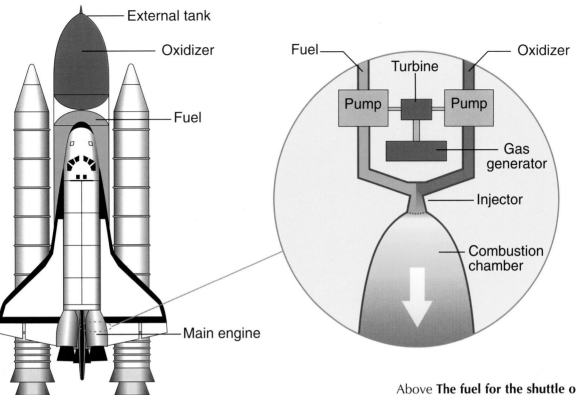

External tank

Oxidizer

Fuel

Main engine

Fuel — Turbine — Oxidizer

Pump

Pump

Gas generator

Injector

Combustion chamber

The combustion process starts when the liquid propellants are injected into the rocket engine. Some propellants, known as hypergolic propellants, will ignite as soon as they come into contact with each other. Non-hypergolic propellants require a separate igniter. Some engines have used spark plugs for this purpose.

Above **The fuel for the shuttle orbiter's three main engines is carried in a large external tank. Fuel and oxidizer are pumped into each engine's combustion chamber. A simple pumping mechanism is shown here. The orbiter's main engines have the most complicated liquid-propellant system ever built.**

Into orbit!

To reach earth orbit, a spacecraft must reach a speed of about 16,800 mph (27,000 kph) and a speed of around 25,000 mph (40,000 kph) to escape the earth's gravity completely for a flight to another planet. The *Apollo* spacecraft that traveled to the moon in 1969 (see page 26) had to reach a speed of nearly 24,000 mph (38,000 kph). One way to achieve such high velocities is by using a succession of rockets mounted one on top of the other. The powerful first-stage rocket has to lift the weight of the entire vehicle off the ground. The second, third, or even fourth rockets are ignited as the previous stage cuts out and falls away. The rocket becomes progressively lighter as each stage separates, so the following stage boosts its velocity even more. Finally, the payload reaches earth orbit or is sent on its trajectory to its destination in space.

This *Ariane 4* rocket has three stages. Attached to the first stage are "strap-on" boosters, which help blast it into space.

NUCLEAR UMBRELLAS

The economy of the former USSR was practically crippled by the cost of keeping pace with the United States in developing new and more powerful nuclear missiles. Here, a submarine-launched missile is paraded through Moscow's Red Square.

The development of more and more powerful rockets in the 1950s was not the result of scientific curiosity. Instead, it was a race between the United States and the USSR to produce a missile that could deliver a nuclear strike at the other country.

At the beginning of the Cold War, in the late 1940s, the United States was the only country in the world that had atomic bombs. But the USSR soon caught up, and by 1953 both countries had developed the even more powerful hydrogen bomb.

"The Beast" is born

The USSR's hydrogen bomb weighed nearly two tons. The challenge that faced their missile designers was to build a rocket capable of delivering this massive payload into the United States. Sergei Korolev, the leader of the Soviet missile program, produced the R7 rocket, which had several small engines clustered around a central core. The U.S. intelligence services code-named this ungainly looking rocket "The Beast." On its first successful test flight in 1957, it traveled 4,000 miles (6,400 km). The USSR had built the first ICBM.

Over the next few decades, the United States and the USSR poured colossal amounts of money and effort into developing missiles that could carry nuclear warheads swiftly and accurately to their targets. In fact, each side's missiles became so powerful and accurate that they effectively cancelled each other out. Neither side could risk attacking the other without being itself wiped out by a counter-strike.

The ICBM is one of the most complicated machines ever made. It has more than 300,000 parts, all of which must function perfectly. It has to work across an extraordinary range of temperatures: the warhead is exposed to a chilly -297°F (-183°C) at the fringes of space and heats to 6,000°F (3,300°C) on reentry into the earth's atmosphere. The missile must also withstand the force of acceleration as it reaches velocities in excess of 3,100 mph (5,000 kph) in less than a minute. It also sways and rolls as it flies, buffeted by the atmosphere.

Multiple independently targetable reentry vehicles (MIRVs)

Before the 1970s, a missile carried a single warhead and could be launched at only one target. MIRVs made it possible for a single missile launch to attack anywhere from three to fourteen different targets. The Minuteman 3, for example, carries three warheads, while the Poseidon submarine-launched missile can be equipped with between ten and fourteen warheads. Each of these may be directed to separate, widely distant targets.

The Minuteman 3, launched from a hardened concrete silo, carries three nuclear warheads, each one aimed at a different target.

HITTING THE TARGET

Each Peacekeeper missile carries ten independently targeted warheads.

A ballistic missile may be launched against a far distant target. How is it guided to its target? In most cases, the missile must receive guidance instructions during the powered phase of its flight, while the engines are still running. Once it reaches the top of its arc above the earth, the motors shut down and the warhead separates from the booster rocket to begin its descent toward the target. At this stage in its flight, it can no longer be guided.

During the powered phase, electronic equipment on board the missile controls the large rocket engines and the smaller steering motors. The smaller rockets will continue to fire for a short time after the main booster rocket has shut down, giving the final, crucial tweaks and nudges to the missile's speed and direction. Once these rockets shut off, the missile's flightpath cannot be altered.

Radio-inertial guidance

Because the missile climbs to a great height during the powered phase of its flight, it does not travel out of sight of ground-based radar. Radar systems constantly measure the position and velocity of the accelerating missile. This information is radioed to a ground-based computer that transmits control orders back to the missile. The disadvantage of this system is that it can be deliberately jammed by the enemy. The radio signal can also be bent and distorted as it passes through clouds or by the exhaust from the missile itself. For these reasons, stellar-inertial guidance systems are preferred for longer-range missiles.

The submarine-launched Trident missile corrects its course during flight by taking an accurate fix on the position of a known star.

Stellar-inertial guidance (SIG)

Mobile missile systems, such as those launched from submarines, are less accurate than fixed land-based systems because their exact location at the time of launch is normally less well known. SIG is designed to compensate for this problem. A computer on board the missile takes a sighting on a star and uses this to determine the missile's position, rather than relying on a radar signal from the ground.

Future navigation system (FANS)

Aircraft, submarines, and spacecraft also use inertial guidance systems. In 1992, eighty-five nations began trials of a new navigation system that would make use of the space technology developed during the Cold War. FANS will make use of twenty-four Russian satellites and twenty-four U.S. satellites. Small computers will be fitted to civilian aircraft to process signals from the satellites, allowing navigation anywhere in the world with pinpoint accuracy.

MISSILE DEFENSES

One of the many ideas that were put forward for a missile defense system. The metal "net" on the nose of the interceptor missile increases the chances of a strike on an incoming enemy missile. This system was tested successfully in 1984.

In 1984, the United States government set up an organization to conduct research into what was called the Strategic Defense Initiative (SDI). SDI, popularly known as Star Wars, was to provide a means of destroying enemy missiles before they could hit their targets, using weapons systems based in space.

One way to destroy an enemy missile after it has been fired would be to hit the warheads as they are falling through outer space, or after they have reentered the atmosphere. Waiting until reentry would be hazardous because the warhead would be close to its target by then and might detonate if hit. Up to a dozen warheads might be released from a single missile, along with a number of decoys designed to confuse ground-based defenses. This would make the real warheads difficult targets to hit.

A better alternative would be to hit the missile while it is still in one piece. The heat of its engines would provide a beacon for an interceptor missile to home in on. However, a fast-burn booster might be used, which would burn out before it could be tracked and targeted. There is also the problem of how an interceptor missile would catch up with an enemy missile already in flight and traveling at its maximum speed. For these reasons, an effective defense system would have to be positioned in orbit and have to employ some kind of beam weapon.

An artist's impression of a space laser being fired at a target from the cargo bay of a shuttle orbiter.

Beam weapons

Beams of electromagnetic radiation in the form of microwaves could be produced by the explosion in space of a small nuclear bomb. These microwaves would be channeled into a very narrow angle and then focused into beams that could be directed to a target in space or on the ground.

The high-energy beams that were being developed for use by SDI could just as easily be used for attack as for defense. A beam weapon that could attack enemy targets, while at the same time providing a defensive shield for a country's own military bases and cities, would give that country an overwhelming advantage.

With the end of the Cold War, the need for SDI was reduced, and the system was never put into operation. However, research has continued into developing a system to protect the United States and its allies from "accidental, unauthorized, and limited ballistic missile attack." The new approach, called Global Protection Against Limited Strikes, is planned to consist of sensors and interceptor missiles based on the ground and in orbit around the earth.

SPACE SPECTACULARS

On October 4, 1957, the USSR fired the starting pistol that began the space race with the launch of *Sputnik 1*. The USSR's success seemed to take everyone by surprise, and people were astounded to think that an artificial object, traveling at a speed of 17,900 mph (28,800 kph), was circling the earth. A month later, the USSR launched *Sputnik 2*. Inside was a dog called Laika, the first animal to reach outer space.

On January 31, 1958, the United States succeeded in getting *Explorer 1* into orbit. The Juno 1 rocket, a modified medium-range rocket was used. On July 29, the National Aeronautics and Space Administration (NASA) was set up to take charge of the U.S. space program.

First human in space

Both the United States and the USSR knew that the country that put the first person into orbit would win an important battle in the war of words between the two countries. In April 1959, the United States selected their first astronauts. Unfortunately, they had no launcher or capsule capable of carrying the men into space.

The launch of *Vostok 1* (top left). Colonel Yuri Gagarin (left) in the capsule that carried him into history as the first human in space.

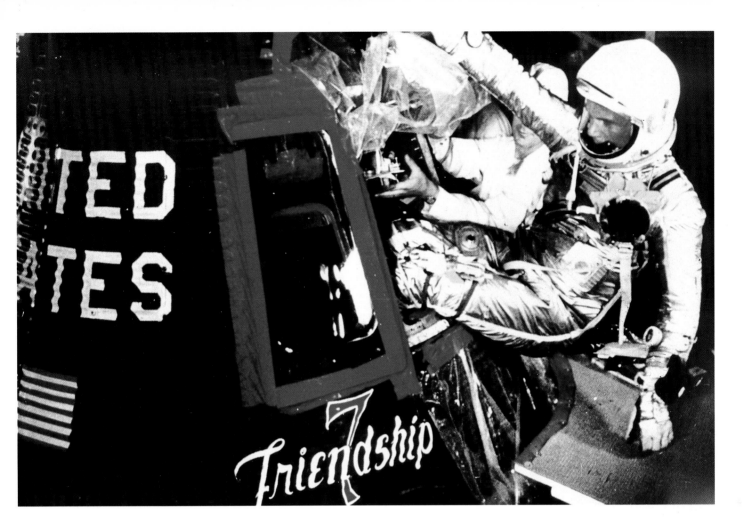

John H. Glenn, the first American astronaut to orbit the earth, climbs into his Mercury space capsule.

On April 12, 1961, the USSR announced that Colonel Yuri Gagarin, aboard his Vostok spacecraft, had successfully gone into orbit. The impact of this achievement was felt around the world. Now the Space Age had truly begun.

Meanwhile, the United States was developing the Mercury capsule. There was no U.S. rocket that could compete with the lifting power of the USSR's launcher, so the capsule was kept small and simple. It weighed just 3,000 pounds (1,360 kg) and was about 6 feet (2m) long and 6 feet (2m) in diameter. One end was covered with a heat shield to protect the capsule and its occupant against the 5,500°F (3,000°C) heat of reentry into the atmosphere.

The Atlas ICBM was used to provide the lifting power needed to put a person into orbit. On February 20, 1962, John H. Glenn became the first American to fly into orbit.

The Sputnik booster

All the Sputnik satellites and the Vostok spacecraft were launched using an R7 rocket, codenamed the SS-6, or Sapwood, by the West. It was originally designed as an ICBM, and its upper stage was modified slightly to hold the Sputnik and Vostok payloads. It had two stages. The first stage consisted of four strap-on booster rockets, which were connected to the second-stage rocket. Both stages used liquid oxygen and paraffin as their propellants and the first-stage motors could provide 220,000 lb (100,000 kg) of thrust.

TO THE MOON

The launch of the *Apollo 11* mission to the moon (above). The mission controllers on Earth (above right) had some nail-biting moments to live through.

In 1961, President John F. Kennedy committed the United States to putting a person on the moon within ten years. U.S. probes mapped the moon's surface to pinpoint suitable landing sites for the planned mission. The Gemini missions gave both astronauts and ground crews the experience they would need for the moon flight. Astronauts practiced maneuvering in space, space walking, and docking with other craft in orbit. In May 1969, Apollo 10 flew within 15 miles (24 km) of the moon's surface. The scene was set for *Apollo 11*.

On July 16, 1969, Neil Armstrong, mission commander, Edwin "Buzz" Aldrin, lunar-module pilot, and Michael Collins, command-module pilot, were strapped into their capsule on top of a three-stage Saturn V rocket that stood 560 feet (107m) high. Powerful F–1 rocket engines generated a takeoff thrust of about 7.6 million pounds (3.45 million kg) as they consumed around 28,000 pounds (12,700 kg) of propellant per second. Finally, the third-stage rocket kicked in to boost the velocity to over 23,600 miles per hour (38,000 km/h) and send *Apollo 11* out of earth orbit and on its way to the moon. Collins separated the command module, *Columbia,* from the third stage and maneuvered it around to dock with the lunar module, *Eagle.*

On July 20, *Eagle* separated from *Columbia,* and Armstrong and Aldrin began the descent to the lunar surface. Some tense moments followed when Armstrong had to guide the lunar module over the cratered and boulder-strewn surface.

Buzz Aldrin walks on the moon (left). Neil Armstrong is seen reflected in Aldrin's helmet visor.

U.S. Navy divers attend the command module after its splashdown in the Pacific Ocean (below).

After landing safely in the Sea of Tranquillity, Armstrong radioed home: "Houston, Tranquillity base here. The *Eagle* has landed."

It was Armstrong who climbed down the ladder of the lunar module and left the first human footprint on the surface of the moon. Fifteen minutes later, Aldrin joined him, and for the next two hours they set up experiments and collected rock samples.

After twenty-one hours on the moon's surface, the upper stage of the lunar module blasted them back to the command module. The historic mission ended on July 24, when the command module splashed down safely in the Pacific Ocean.

A new view of home

The 1968 flight of *Apollo 8*, which was the first to orbit the moon, beamed back one of the most historic photos ever taken, showing Earth alone in the icy blackness of space. Later, *Apollo 14* astronaut Alan Shepard had this to say: "I realized up there that our planet is not infinite. It's fragile ... We look pretty vulnerable in the darkness of space."

DOWN-TO-EARTH APPLICATIONS

In 1989, NASA conducted a study that examined in detail as many as 250 commercial uses of space-program technology. It is estimated that more than 350,000 jobs had been created from space research developments. A few of the more unusual examples of space technology that have become part of our everyday lives are described below.

Permanent fabrics

During the Apollo program, NASA technicians looked for ways to improve spacesuit fabrics. They wanted a hard-wearing and flame-resistant material that was also thin, lightweight, and flexible. The fabric they used had fiberglass yarn woven into it. It was then coated with a plastic material called Teflon for added strength and durability and to make it waterproof. More uses were soon found for the fabric. A heavier version of it is used as roofing for an airport terminal in Saudi Arabia, and for zoos, sports stadiums, and shopping malls in the United States and Canada. Weight for weight, the fabric is stronger than steel and is considerably lighter as well.

Ships that are required to carry out their operations over a particular point on the seabed are able to hold their position using a computer-controlled system developed for the U.S. space program.

Deep-sea drill-ships

Space technology has been used to solve problems in deep-water oil-drilling operations. For deep-water drilling, an oil drill-ship is used. A "marine riser"—a cylindrical steel tube usually about a foot and a half (0.5 m) in diameter—connects the drill-ship to the ocean floor, far below. The drilling equipment is lowered to the well through this riser. The riser is not rigid but is held in position at the well and at the ship by strong cables.

Satellites can be used to keep track of major pollution, such as the oil slick shown here as a bright swirl on the waters of the Gulf of Oman. This photograph was taken from the *Atlantis* shuttle orbiter.

The ship must be held in position above the well, often for months. Any drifting might snap the riser, disrupting operations and polluting the ocean with huge quantities of oil. This is where space technology comes in. If a spacecraft has to hold a certain position, computer-directed control thrusters are fired, adjusting speed and direction as necessary. The same techniques can be used to hold the drill-ship in position over the well-site.

A small, battery-powered beacon is placed on the seabed at the drilling site. This emits a sound signal that is picked up by receivers, called hydrophones, on the hull of the drill-ship. The hydrophones relay information to a computer on the ship, which analyzes the signals to determine whether a course correction is needed. If it is, then the computer operates the ship's engines to move it, until the signals from the beacon indicate that the ship is once again in position.

Lasering pollution

Accidental leaks of toxic gases can be a problem in a space station, just as they can be to people living near a factory. A team of U.S. scientists has adapted a spaceship's laser-powered, toxic-gas analyzer into a portable device called EcoScan, which health officials can use to identify industrial polluters.

BATTLEFIELD MISSILES

There is no doubt that the biggest application of all for rockets has been in wars. As the Chinese discovered 900 years ago, a rocket barrage can have a devastating effect on an enemy. A rocket that can be guided right to its target is even more deadly. Missile technology has moved on considerably since the days of fireworks tied to arrows, and it now plays a vital role in all forms of combat—on land, on sea, and in the air. We have looked at ICBMs, the biggest of the military rockets (see page 18). Here, we will take a look at some of the smaller battlefield weapons.

Tactical missiles

Tactical missiles, or battlefield missiles, include rockets and a wide variety of other weapons. The U.S. Lance missile is light enough to be transported by helicopter. It has a range of around 81 miles (130 km). It is equipped with an inertial navigation system and can be fitted with a nuclear warhead. Soviet-built Scud missiles, with a range of about 168 miles (270 km) were used by Iraq against the Coalition Forces in the Gulf War of 1991.

An air-to-air missile is launched from a French Mirage Rafale aircraft.

Close-support missiles

These missiles are designed to be fired from a military aircraft against a target on the ground, to provide back-up for infantry and other ground forces. They can be controlled by radio commands after firing and can be powered by either jet engines or rocket motors. By using close-support missiles, aircraft can launch attacks against enemy targets while remaining out of range of enemy missile defenses. They can also avoid immediate attack by enemy fighter aircraft.

A U.S. Patriot missile is fired from its launcher. Patriots were used in combat during the Gulf War in 1991.

Air-to-air missiles

These missiles, such as the Sidewinder, Sparrow, and Phoenix, are designed to be fired from a fighter aircraft against flying targets, such as enemy fighters and bombers, transport aircraft, or cruise missiles.

Surface-to-air missiles

Surface-to-air missiles are designed to be fired from the ground or a ship against enemy aircraft and missiles. The U.S. Patriot system was used during the Gulf War to intercept incoming Iraqi Scud missiles. A Patriot unit is mobile and consists of the missile launcher, an engagement center, and a radar tracking center. These allow the system to lock onto a target and guide a missile to destroy it.

GUIDANCE SYSTEMS

Modern missiles can be equipped with sophisticated guidance systems to ensure that they reach their target. One of these systems is beam riding, which is often used by surface-to-air missiles. A radar transmitter produces a beam that antennae in the missile can lock onto. A control system on the missile checks that the missile is receiving the beam equally at all of its antennae. If it is, the missile is on course and the control system does nothing. If the control system senses a variation in the intensity of the beam among the antennae, it means the missile has strayed off course. The control system then takes the appropriate action to get the missile back on course. Beam-riding systems allow the ground controller to fire and control several missiles simultaneously.

Command guidance

In a command-guidance system, an early-warning radar flashes a signal to a target-tracking radar when it detects an enemy target. An intercepting missile is then launched automatically on a signal from the computer. A missile-tracking radar and the target-tracking radar feed information to the command computer. This in turn sends signals to the missile, directing it on a collision course with the target.

Modern combat aircraft are fitted with sophisticated electronic equipment to guide their missiles to their targets with great accuracy.

The big drawback with both beam-riding and command-guidance systems is their sensitivity to interference and jamming, known as electronic countermeasures. For example, the target might release small missiles ahead of itself. These shower tiny pieces of aluminum foil that confuse the radar equipment.

A Milan command-guidance missile is launched from the back of an armored vehicle.

Homing missiles

Missiles also use a variety of homing-guidance systems. In a passive homing system, the missile senses and locks onto a source of energy from the target, for example, infrared radiation from the hot tailpipe of a jet. The missile's onboard computer tracks the target, sending course correction commands as necessary to the missile's guidance system.

Active homing is used for long-range attacks. The missile carries a radar transmitter that transmits an energy pulse to the target and a receiver to detect the echo that is reflected back. This information is fed into the onboard computer. During its climb and the early part of the flight, the missile can be guided from the ground or an aircraft. Once it approaches the target, its own internal system can take over.

The cruise missile's terrain recognition radar "reads" the ground it flies over and compares it to a map carried in its onboard computer, which then makes any necessary course corrections.

Terrain recognition

Terrain recognition is the system used in cruise missiles. A previously prepared radar map of the ground over which the missile will fly to the target is stored in the missile's computer system before it is launched. As the missile flies toward its target, its radar unit constantly compares what it detects with the radar map in the computer and makes any corrections that are necessary. Cruise missiles are not actually rockets because they are powered by jet engines.

SPACE STATIONS

Skylab, the first U.S. space station, was launched using a Saturn V rocket. It could house a crew of three people.

A space station is a large structure in space in which people can live for long periods. There, experiments can be carried out in micro-gravity conditions, and the medical effects of long periods of weightlessness can be studied. The first space station was the 20-ton *Salyut 1*, launched in 1971 by the USSR.

In May 1973, the United States launched its first experimental space station, *Skylab*. Three three-man crews occupied *Skylab* for a total of 171 days and 13 hours and carried out as many as 300 scientific and technical experiments. The space station remained in orbit for more than six years, until it disintegrated in the atmosphere, scattering debris over the Indian Ocean and parts of Western Australia.

The International Space Station

The United States, Russia, the European Space Agency (ESA), Canada, Italy, and Japan are all involved in the $30-billion *Alpha* project, to build the world's first orbiting international laboratory. This marks the beginning of a new era of cooperation in space research.

An artist's impression of the International Space Station, *Alpha*, in orbit. Solar panels will provide most of the power for the station. Shuttle orbiters will ferry crew and supplies from Earth.

In 1996, Russia announced that it had finished building the 22-ton functional cargo block (FCB), the module that will form the core of *Alpha*. The FCB has been jointly designed and built by the Russians and the Boeing Company of the United States. It is due to be launched into earth orbit at the end of 1997. By 1998, three space-station modules, including a U.S.-built laboratory module, will be attached to it, and scientists will be able to begin experimentation and research. The space station is due to be completed early in the twenty-first century.

The FCB will be fitted with special adapters to allow docking of the different spacecraft from the countries involved in the project. It will carry equipment to provide energy for the station and will also be used to store scientific equipment and a supply of rocket fuel.

The station will be completed by the attachment of a Canadian remote manipulator system, an ESA facility, several modules providing accommodation, and research facilities and solar panels. The launch and assembly of all the components will need more than seventy flights by spacecraft from the countries involved. The completed station will measure 360 feet by 290 feet (110 m x 88 m). It will weigh 500 tons and house a crew of six.

THE SPACE SHUTTLE

Separation of solid-fuel boosters

External fuel tank falls away

Shuttle orbiter goes into orbit

Crew carries out its mission

Boosters parachute down for recovery

External fuel tank burns up in atmosphere

Launch

A shuttle mission begins with the launch, using the shuttle orbiter's main engines and the solid-fuel boosters. Two minutes after take-off, the solid-fuel boosters separate and parachute down to the Atlantic Ocean where they are recovered for reuse. Eight minutes after launch, the external fuel tank is jettisoned to burn up in the atmosphere. The orbiter goes into orbit and the crew can carry out its mission, which may involve placing satellites in orbit.

The Space Shuttle Transportation System (SSTS), to give it its full name, was one of the first attempts to make space travel less expensive. By developing a reusable spacecraft, the United States hoped to reduce the cost of putting satellites into orbit.

Four shuttle orbiters were built in the 1980s. One, *Challenger*, was destroyed in a mid-air explosion shortly after launch because of a fault in one of the solid-fuel boosters. All seven of the crew died. A fifth orbiter, *Endeavor*, flew for the first time in 1992.

The shuttle orbiter itself is about the size of a DC-9 airliner. It is designed to carry a crew of seven, along with almost 66,000 pounds (30,000 kg) of equipment, into earth orbit. The weight of the orbiter at takeoff, which varies slightly with each mission, is around 4.5 million pounds (2 million kg).

The shuttle orbiter is boosted into orbit using its liquid fuel rockets plus a pair of solid-fuel booster rockets. The solid-fuel boosters separate from the shuttle and fall back to earth about two minutes after launch, when it has reached a height of about 28 miles (45 km). The boosters are recovered so that they can be reused. Eight minutes after launch, when it is about 68 miles (110 km) up, the space shuttle's huge external fuel tank falls away, and the main engines cut out.

Main engines fire to bring orbiter down

Orbiter reenters the atmosphere

Orbiter glides back without engines

Pilot maneuvers to adjust orbiter's speed and course

Orbiter lands

Maneuvering engines fire to position the space shuttle in orbit. At the end of its mission, the orbiter fires retro-rockets to take it back into the atmosphere and it glides, without power, down to its landing strip.

Other shuttle vehicles

Several other nations have worked to develop their own shuttle vehicles. The Soviet shuttle, *Buran,* looked so much like the U.S. design that there were rumors that Soviet engineers had somehow got hold of the U.S. plans. Unlike the U.S. orbiter, *Buran* carried only maneuvering engines. The launcher used four large liquid-fuel boosters with the main engines in a recoverable pod in the base of the external tank. *Buran* made only one uncrewed flight, in 1988. The program was eventually discontinued through lack of funding.

In the mid-1980s, the ESA began work on the *Hermes* shuttle, which was intended to carry four astronauts and a small payload to orbit and back. Again, rising costs saw the project cancelled in 1994. Japan's National Space Development Agency is currently developing the H-2 Orbital Plane Experiment (HOPE). HOPE will initially be used as an unmanned cargo vehicle, but crewed flights are planned for the future.

When the mission has been carried out, the crew closes the cargo bay doors and fires the main engines for about fives minutes. This slows down the orbiter, and the pilot turns it to enter the atmosphere belly first. The pilot and commander fly the orbiter back to the Kennedy Space Center, curving back and forth to adjust its speed. On the ground, the orbiter is towed to a special hanger to be made ready for its next mission.

A COST-EFFECTIVE FUTURE

Voyager 2 flies past Saturn. Unmanned space probes transmit information about space and the planets of the solar system back to Earth.

The last mission to the moon flew in 1972. Since that time, no human has left Earth orbit. The Space Age that seemed to be getting off to such a flying start in the 1960s seems to have fizzled out. Why should this be?

It is extraordinarily expensive to put a payload into space. Every time the space shuttle is launched, it costs approximately $1 billion. In the 1960s, the U.S. government spent 4 percent of the national budget every year for ten years putting people on the moon.

The main reason for spending such colossal sums of money was propaganda. Until the beginning of the 1990s, when the Cold War between the United States and the former USSR ended, each country had been determined to outdo the other in the space race. Now, rocket engineers are more concerned with efficiency than with making headlines.

X-33

The X–33 Single-Stage-to-Orbit (SSTO) Reusable Launch Vehicle (RLV) is a half-scale version of the craft that could replace the space shuttles when they are retired from service about 2012. When it is built, the X–33 will be the first major new U.S. spacecraft for twenty-five years. If it is successful, it should lead to the building of the VentureStar, which will take off straight up like a rocket and land like a plane.

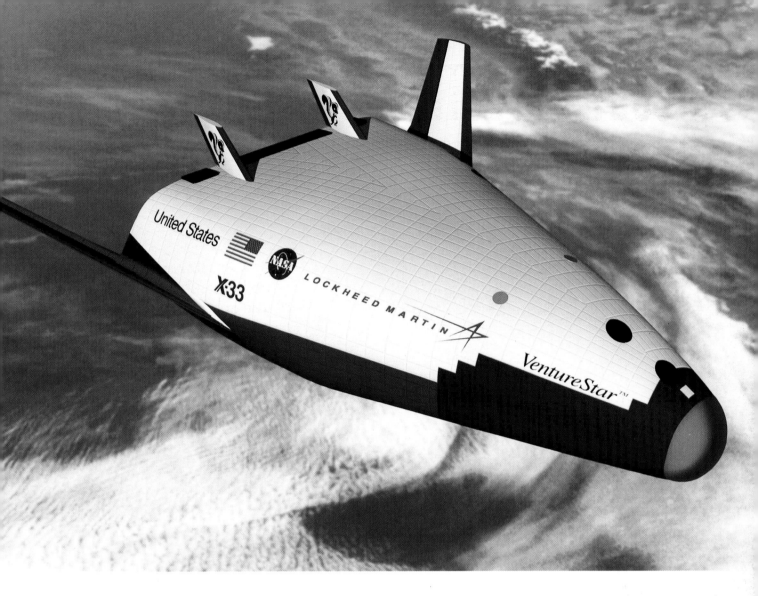

The space shuttle sheds its expensive boosters and fuel tank on the way up, but the VentureStar will employ a new type of engine, known as a linear aerospike. This will be powerful enough to propel it into orbit without boosters. A wedge-shaped "lifting body" fuselage and tiny wings will provide lift in the atmosphere when the ship flies back to land. The design is highly efficient, keeping the craft much cooler during reentry than the existing shuttle orbiter.

If everything goes according to plan, then the new craft could blast into space every few days, requiring only a small number of maintenance people to turn it around between missions. As a result, the cost of putting freight into orbit could drop from more than $9,000 a pound (0.5kg) on the space shuttle to roughly $900 on the VentureStar. Some experts have predicted that it will not be long before ordinary people will be able to buy tickets for space flights.

An artist's impression of the VentureStar in orbit. This reusable spacecraft is planned to replace the space shuttle at the beginning of the twenty-first century.

JAPAN: THE NEW PLAYER

HOPE, the planned Japanese shuttle vehicle, will be used to ferry supplies to the International Space Station.

In 1995, Japan tested a prototype orbiter, suspending it by cables from a helicopter and releasing it high above a desert landing strip in southern Australia. Test landings of the Automatic Landing Flight Experiment Plane (ALFLEX) continued for several weeks, with the 20-foot (6-m), 1,650-pound (750-kg) craft being controlled each time by a computer and satellite signals. The successful tests meant that Japan could start work on its first unmanned shuttle, called HOPE, due for launch in 2000. Japan plans to use HOPE to ship supplies and equipment to and from the International Space Station, which is also due for launch about 2000 (see page 34).

With its strong economy and technological skills, Japan is expected to overtake Russia in space exploration in the near future. Funding for the Japanese space program will almost certainly grow over the next ten to fifteen years. However, as Masanori Homma of the National Space Development Agency of Japan points out, "The next question is how to use that technology."

Japan's H–II rocket has been launched successfully four times since 1994, but each launch costs $170 million. This makes it too expensive to compete in the growing worldwide market for commercial launch vehicles. As a result, the H–II is being redesigned into a much cheaper version called the H–IIA, which will cost about $77 million to launch. The first test launch of the new rocket is planned for the year 2000.

Japanese Moon shots

In 1997, Japan plans to launch a probe to the moon. It will drop three devices equipped with sensors on to the lunar surface, to gather information on the moon's structure. In 2003, the Japanese plan to land an unmanned spacecraft on the moon and put satellites into lunar orbit to map the surface of the moon in detail.

The Japanese space program is unusual in that it has entirely commercial and peaceful aims. The knowledge gained could be put to military use, but the law of Japan forbids the use of space technology for military purposes.

Japan's H–II rocket is powerful enough to put a 4,400-pound (2,000-kg) satellite into earth orbit. It is due to be replaced by the more economical H–IIA rocket.

SPACE FOR EVERYONE?

In 1996, an unusual competition was launched in St. Louis, Missouri. The "X Prize," as it is called, will be awarded to the first team safely to launch and land a rocket capable of carrying three people to an altitude of 62 miles (100 km). They must make the flight twice, with a gap of no more than two weeks between flights. The reward for this achievement will be $10 million.

The contest is being organized by The X Prize Foundation, with the aim of encouraging development of commercial space travel and tourism. One of the favorites to win the X Prize is American Burt Rutan, creator of the Voyager, the first aircraft to fly non-stop around the world, but it is likely to attract pilots, inventors, and aerospace researchers from all over the world.

A spectacular picture of a star's death photographed by the Hubble Space Telescope. The future will bring new and exciting discoveries about the universe.

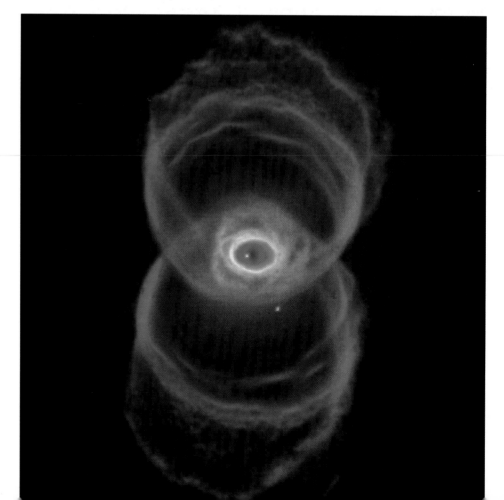

NASA sees the contest as a pioneering effort that could open up new possibilities for space research. It could also be the start of a profitable space-tourism industry, offering everyone the chance to go into space. Reusable spacecraft, such as the X–33 (see page 38), would return to earth, refuel in much the same way as an aircraft, and quickly be ready to return to space, saving time and money.

Some time in the twenty-first century, a human may look out over the landscape of Mars for the very first time.

Space: the endless frontier

In the forty years since the launch of *Sputnik 1*, rockets have pushed our space probes to the farthest reaches of the solar system. In the twenty-first century, new satellites and space probes, space observatories and telescopes, space stations, and, perhaps, a crewed flight to Mars will open up further frontiers and bring us new knowledge and fresh experiences. In a letter to the author H.G. Wells, written in 1932, Robert Goddard said:

"There can be no thought of finishing, for 'aiming at the stars' ... is a problem to occupy generations. So that no matter how much progress one makes, there is always the thrill of just beginning ..."

DATE CHART

1903 Russian Konstantin E. Tsiolkovsky describes how rockets could be used for space exploration.

1926 American Robert H. Goddard flies the world's first liquid-fuel rocket.

1945 German Werner von Braun and his team perfect the V2 rocket.

1957 The former USSR launches the first satellite, *Sputnik 1*. It remains in orbit for three months. *Sputnik 2* carries the dog, Laika, into space.

1958 The United States launches *Explorer 1*, its first satellite. NASA is founded.

1959 The USSR launches *Luna 2*, the first object from Earth to reach the surface of the moon.

1960 *Sputnik 5* carries two dogs, Strelka and Belka, into orbit.

1961 Cosmonaut Yuri A. Gargarin becomes the first human in space.

1962 John H. Glenn becomes the first American astronaut to orbit the earth.

Mariner 2 is launched and flies past Venus, the first probe to reach another planet.

1963 Cosmonaut Valentina Tereshkova becomes the first woman in space.

1965 Cosmonaut Alexei A. Leonov takes the first space walk. U.S. astronauts make 206 orbits around earth, proving that humans can stay in space long enough to fly to the moon.

1966 Soviet *Luna 9* soft-lands on the moon. Soviet *Venera 3* crashes on Venus, the first spacecraft to reach the surface of another planet.

1968 The unmanned Soviet *Zond 5* orbits the moon and returns to Earth. U.S. astronauts make the first manned flight around the moon in *Apollo 8*.

1969 *Apollo 11* astronauts carry out the first manned lunar landing.

1971 Soviet *Salyut 1* space station is launched. U.S. *Mariner 9* becomes the first spacecraft to orbit another planet, Mars.

1973 U.S. *Skylab Workshop* is launched.

1975 *Apollo 18* and Soviet *Soyuz 19* dock in earth orbit, the first international spacecraft rendezvous.

1976 *Viking 2* lands on the Plain of Utopia, Mars, where it discovers water frost.

1977 First test flight of the space shuttle.

1978 U.S. *Pioneer Venus 2* drops five probes toward the surface of the planet.

1979 U.S. *Voyager 1* and 2 fly past Jupiter. U.S. *Pioneer 11* takes the first close-up photographs of Saturn.

1981 First orbital test flight of the shuttle orbiter, *Columbia*.

1982 Soviet *Venera 13* makes the first analysis of soil on Venus.

1983 Sally K. Ride becomes the first American woman to travel in space, in the *Challenger* orbiter.

1984 Bruce McCandless takes the first untethered space walk using the new Manned Maneuvering Unit (MMU).

1985 Maiden flight of the fourth shuttle orbiter, *Atlantis*.

1986 *Voyager 2* passes Uranus. *Challenger* explodes shortly after takeoff, killing all seven crew members.

1987 USSR launches the new Energiya rocket. Cosmonaut Yuri V. Romanenko returns from space station *Mir* after a record 326 days in space.

1988 *Discovery* lifts off on the first crewed flight since the Challenger disaster.

1989 *Voyager 2* passes Neptune.

1990 A satellite is put into orbit using a Pegasus rocket fired from a B-52 bomber.

1994 Japan launches its first H–II rocket.

1995 Cosmonaut Valeriy Polyakov returns to earth after a record-breaking 438-day mission aboard *Mir*.

1996 The VentureStar proposal is given the go-ahead.

GLOSSARY

acceleration Increase in speed.

antenna A wire or rod used for radiating or receiving radio waves.

artificial Produced by humans.

artillery Large guns or cannons.

astronaut A person who flies in space.

attitude The orientation of a spacecraft in relation to some fixed point, such as the horizon, giving the direction in which it is traveling.

booster The first-stage rocket of a missile or spacecraft launcher.

capsule The part of a spacecraft that holds the crew.

Cold War The period of tension and hostility between the United States and the USSR and their allies, which lasted from the late 1940s until the late 1980s.

combustion chamber The chamber in a rocket motor where the oxidizer and propellant are ignited.

command module The part of a spacecraft containing the crew and the main control systems.

corps A division of an army.

cosmonaut The Russian term for an astronaut.

dock To connect two or more spacecraft in space.

gravity The force of attraction between objects.

gyro-controlled Controlled by a gyroscope.

gyroscope A device with a spinning wheel. When the wheel is in motion, the device continues to point in the same direction. Gyroscopes are used in missile guidance systems.

habitable Capable of being lived in.

heat shields Devices that protect spacecraft from the heat of reentry into the earth's atmosphere.

ignite To catch fire or set fire to.

igniter The part of a motor that sets the fuel alight.

inertial guidance A system in missiles and spacecraft that works out their position.

infrared radiation Part of the range of waves called the electromagnetic spectrum (EMS). Light rays—waves that we can see—are part of the EMS.

interceptor A missile used to prevent an enemy missile or aircraft from reaching its target.

intercontinental Between the continents.

lunar Of the moon.

lunar module The craft used to carry astronauts from a spacecraft to the moon and back again.

micro-gravity Very low gravity. Weightlessness.

military Of soldiers or warfare; the army.

missions Tasks or duties a person or group is sent to do.

molecules Very small particles.

orbit The path a spacecraft follows around the earth or another body in space under the influence of gravity.

orbiter The reusable spacecraft that carries the crew on its mission in earth orbit.

patents Grants to inventors for the sole right to make or use their inventions.

payload The useful cargo, including crew and equipment, that is lifted into space by a rocket.

probes Unmanned spacecraft that are equipped to find out information about space and transmit it back to earth.

radar A method for detecting the position of an object using radio waves.

retro-rockets Rockets that are used to reduce the velocity of a spacecraft.

rocketeer A person interested in the science and technology of rockets.

satellite A device that orbits the earth. It is also used to mean any natural body that orbits a planet. The moon is a satellite of the earth.

sensors Devices that receive signals and respond to them.

spark plugs Devices in engines that ignite the fuel.

stratosphere A layer of the earth's atmosphere.

thrust Push with force.

thrusters Small rocket engines used for correcting the position of a spacecraft.

trajectory The flight path of a missile or spacecraft.

turbine A kind of engine with curved blades turned by the action of a fluid or gas passing through it.

vacuum A region containing no air.

velocity Speed and direction of motion.

warhead The part of a missile that contains the explosives.

FIND OUT MORE

Books to Read

Blackman, Steven. *Space Travel* (Technology Craft Topics). Danbury, CT: Franklin Watts, 1993.
Hawkes, Nigel. *Space and Aircraft* (New Technology). New York: 21st Century Books, 1994.
Kettelkamp, Larry. *Living in Space*. New York: Morrow Junior Books, 1993.
Parker, Steve. *Satellites* (20th Century Inventions). Austin, TX: Raintree Steck-Vaughn, 1997.
Vogt, Gregory. *The Space Shuttle* (Missions in Space). Brookfield, CT: Millbrook Press, 1991.

Places to visit

National Air and Space Museum
6th Street and Independence Avenue SW
Washington, DC 20560
(203) 357-2700

Franklin Institute Science Museum and Planetarium
20th and Benjamin Franklin Parkway
Philadelphia, PA 19203
(215) 448-1200

INDEX